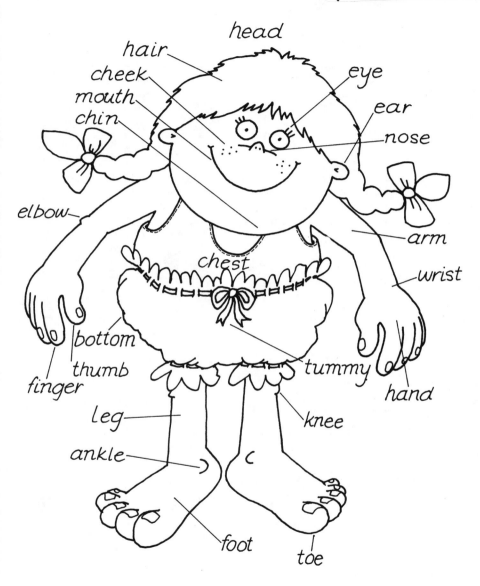

head

hair

cheek

mouth

chin

eye

ear

nose

elbow

arm

chest

wrist

bottom

thumb

finger

tummy

hand

leg

knee

ankle

foot

toe

Aa

apple

acrobat

ant

ax

airport

I am an acrobat.

So am I.

Aa

a
about
after
again
all
along
also
always
am
an
and
another
any
are
around
as
ask
at
away

Dotted guidelines are provided as here on every page so that the child (or parent) can cut own Index edge. This was done in order to keep cost of Dictionary to a minimum.

Aa

Aa

about
all
add
abigil

Bb

Bb

back
be
because
been
before
best
better
big
book
brother
but
by

black
blue
brown

Bb

Bb

Cc

cat coat cup

computer cake chair

I can carry my cat in my coat.

Cc

call
came
can
can't
car
carry
children
come
could

Cc

Cc

Dd

Dd

Dad
Daddy
day
did
do
dollar
don't
down

Dd

Dd

Dd

Ee

egg   elephant   earphones

engine

Eddie Elephant
eats eight eggs
every day.

Ee

each
eat
eight 8
eleven 11
end
even
ever
every

Ee

Ee

Ee

Ff

Ff

family
fast
father
few
find
first
five   5
food
for
found
four   4
friend
from

Ff

Ff

Gg

gate

glasses

goat

garden

giant

In Giggling Gertie's garden
is Giggling Gertie's goat.
What is that he's eating?
Giggling Gertie's coat!

Gg

gave
get
girl
give
go
goes
going
good
got
Grandma
Grandpa

gray
green

Gg

Gg

Gg

Hh

house

half an apple

horse

hat

HOSPITAL

I have to hop home.

Hh

had
has
he
head
heard
help
her
here
him
his
home
hop
how

Hh

Hh

Hh

Ii

insect

igloo

ice cream

intersection

invisible ink

iron

I am eating an invisible ice cream!

Ii

I
if
in
inside
into
is
it

Ii

Ii

Jj

jacket	jam	jeep
jet	Joker	jug

I love jam and jelly.

Jj

jump
just

Kk

kitchen

kangaroo

kennel

kite

kitten

knife

My kitten likes its kennel.

Kk

keep
knew
know

Ll

light

letter

lion

lollipop

lamb

leaf

Lambs don't like lollipops.

LI

last
left
let
life
like
little
live
long
look

LI

LI

LI

Mm

mouse   man   matches

marmalade   money   milk

My mouse likes marmalade and milk.

Mm

made
make
many
map
me
men
might
Mom
Mommy
more
morning
most
mother
much
must
my

Miss
Mr.
Mrs.
Ms.

Mm

Mm

Mm

Nn

numbers

nurse

necklace

needle

TV NEWS

New Zealand

I am the nurse, and with this needle...

No, no, no!

Nn

name
never
new
next
night
nine 9
no
not
November
now

Nn

Nn

Oo

Oo

of
off
Oh
old
on
once
one   1
only
open
or
other
our
out
over

orange

Oo

Oo

Pp

poison

Paste

pen

pie

"Post Office"

paint

If you want some pie, say please!

Please.

Pp

people
place
play
put

pink
purple

Pp

Pp

Pp

Qq

Queen

quail

Quack quack

quilt

Not many words start with q.

Quite right.

Qq

quart
question mark ?
quick
quiet
quite
quiz

Rr

rabbit

radio

rain

Railway Station

RULES
Do not run around the pool.
Do not jump into the pool.

Round and round
the rugged rocks
the ragged rascal ran.

Rr

ran
read
right
road
room
round
run

red

Rr

Rr

Rr

Rr

Ss

snake

spoon

salad

sandwich

scissors

seesaw

Shoe Shop

OPEN

Seashells for sale

She sells seashells on the seashore.

Ss

said
sat
saw
say
sea
see
seven 7
school
she
should
side
six 6
small
so
some
something
sometimes
soon
still
sure

Ss

Ss

Ss

Tt

Tt

take	told
tell	too
ten 10	took
than	town
that	tried
the	try
their	twelve 12
them	twenty 20
then	two 2
there	
these	
they	
thing	
think	
this	
thought	
three 3	
through	
time	
to	
today	

Tt

Uu

umbrella

ukelele

university

upside down

universe

Uncle's ukelele won't get wet under the umbrella.

Uu

under
until
up
us

Uu

Vv

van

violets in a vase

violin

vacuum cleaner

Color these vegetables very carefully.

Vv
very

Vv

Ww

watch	window	walrus
woman	wool	whale

1. 2. 3. 4. 5.

Which watch would you wear?
Answer: I would wear number ____

Ww

walk
want
was
water
way
we
well
went
were
what
when
where
which
while
who
will
with
won't
work
would

white

Xx

X-ray

xylophone

Not many words start with X.

Xx

Xx

Yy

yacht

YOGURT

Color the yolk of the egg yellow.

yawn

Yy

year
yes
you
your

yellow

Zz

Zz

zebra
zero
zip

Words I can spell

Words I can spell

Words I can spell

Words I can spell

Words I can spell